# Embolden

SONEE SINGH

First published in Australia in 2022
by MMH Press
Waikiki, WA 6169

www.mmhpress.com

Cover design by: Jennifer Dinsdale
Interior design by: Ida Jansson

NATIONAL LIBRARY OF AUSTRALIA

A catalogue record for this work is available from the National Library of Australia

National Library of Australia Catalogue-in-Publication data:
Embolden/Sonee Singh

ISBN (Hardback)
ISBN (Paperback)

*For My Aaji*
*Who*
*Always*
*Holds my Hand*
*From Beyond*

*We have lived* through some of the toughest times our generation has had to endure. Moments of pause and challenges are the universe's way of letting us know that we must pivot or redirect in some way. Challenges are ways our spirit deals with ascension—a rise in energy that elevates us.

How do we move forward? We make the best of what we have, adapting to our circumstances. Some days are better than others but we persevere. At times, we may take a few steps backwards but we don't give up. We may need to gather a better perspective, learn a lesson or two, but we forge ahead. We embody what has happened, embrace and accept it, and this is what is next.

Recognizing that made me feel emboldened. Poetry helped me reach new heights that I didn't think possible. It filled me in ways few things have been able to. According to Merriam Webster, Embolden means the following:

To impart boldness or courage to

To instill with boldness, courage or resolution enough to overcome timidity or misgiving

I needed to distinguish between embolden and empower. While embolden means to motivate, empower means to give someone strength or confidence to do something. While I felt strong, the overriding feeling was of inspiration.

The theme for embolden was a natural result of having embodied what was happening to make sense of the strangeness of it all and embracing it to make the best of it. Embolden came as I realized that this was not a status quo but a necessary step to move on to the next stage of my life. This is a transition and it is temporary, and in strange ways, it is preparing us for what comes next, making us resilient.

These poems are organized into five sections, each according to a particular area of spiritual significance. The numerology of five represents change. I wrote these poems to reflect numerous ways and methods that bring us connection and help us feel inspired by the world around us.

# Connection

One thing leads to another

We don't exist in a vacuum

Or a silo

Our actions have consequences

One step to the next

Everything matters

Cycles of life and death that result from suffering

Karma perpetuates as long as we suffer

Three evils of ignorance, hate, and desire

Everything can liberate us

Teaching us to tap into our resources

Our intuition

# Objects & Places

Knowledge, lore, magic, metaphor, mythology

# Fortress

I live in a fortress

Like a bat

More comfortable in the dark


Laden with my

Thoughts

Fears

Illusions


Yet I feel

Empty

Forlorn

Desolate


Something is missing

Is it just beyond those walls?

What's behind them?

Can I tear them down?

I am pulled by

Boredom

Routine

Curiosity


I break away

One by one

Chisel by chisel

I loosen a brick


A ray filters through

Brightness!

Inspiration!

Motivation!

I break more

And more

And more

And more


Until I am

Blinded

Filled

Flooded


By shining light

# Bubble

Don't push back

Let it out

Let it be


Not you

It builds up

It takes shape


Fancy and carefree

Let it bubble

Let it burst


In awe of every trick

Every drop

Every oddity

Always separate

Part of your experience

Part of your memory


Not you

Part of your history

Part of your future


Definitely not you

Watch it grow

Like a balloon filled with air


Up and up, it rises

Up and up, it goes


Until we can see it no more

Let it bubble

Let it burst

# Carnelian

The orange wonder

Balancing our creation

Cleanses everything

Including itself

Restoring neutrality

In all things

# Emerald auralite

Amethyst and prasiolite coming together

Amplifying the highest of energies

When it seems all is lost

All fights against hope

Deep level healing wafts in

Into the heart and spirit

Grasping our tissues

To manifest our desires

An electrical charge

To the soul

# Magnet

Polar opposites working in conjunction

To draw in treasures

All kinds of abundance

Wishes and dreams


Bringing to you

Intentions you set

The magnetic action of golden healer quartz

Manifesting all we desire

# Egypt

I heeded its call

To infuse me

With its deep wisdom

Its ancient spirits

Toth tapped me with his knowledge

Sekhmet destroyed the demons I held

Hathor lovingly nourished me back to myself

Every vibration of its sand

Every drop of its water

Every touch of its wind

Satiating my yearning

Caressing me back to life

# Where I am

I am exactly where I need to be

Surrounded by whom I need most

White tiger guards my intuition

Orange tiger guides with earthly signals

Sekhmet destroys and rebuilds

Hathor nurtures me with love

Mystics are robed in gray and divine blue

A yellow rose marks the path of ascension

Ruby red crystals stud the edge

Forming a supportive web

I claim back my power

At the exact time

In the exact place

I am

Where I am

Meant to be

# Energy of a place

I sit quietly pretending to read
Really, I send out tendrils
Sensing the energy of the space

My core picks up signals
There is a density
Collecting in the energy of the place

From disappointment and sadness
Or frustration and perhaps anger
Heating the energy of the space

People expected who didn't come
Loneliness and monotony weighing the passing days
Disturbing the energy of the place

Sadness hangs thick like a fog

People wade through it in slow motion

Clouding the energy of the space


The afflicted in dire need to remove the darkness

And infuse instead with love

Radiating the energy of place


As I continue to sit quietly

I send out healing rays

Clearing the energy of the space


Filling it with light

Spreading it with hope and healing

Creating energy in the place

# Map

Is there such a thing as destiny
An ethereal map that guides us
Predetermined steps we must take
On this quest we call life

There is a bit of destiny
A contract our soul signed
To learn specific life lessons
During this incarnation

We have free will to explore our ways
Trace our own grid
Learn the lesson in this life
Or another

Intersecting lives
Like roads crisscrossing at an intersection
Presenting us a choice
To turn this way or that

At times we speed through
When we could have gone slow
It may make us stumble
But we eventually come back from the detour

Time is not of essence
The globe is eternal
Incarnation will reappear
Until we have pinpointed all the spots

Our soul wanted to mark on the globe
Creating an ever-changing diagram
Marking with our free will
Mapping one life after another

# Agni

A fire raged
Flames scorched their way

Charcoal remnants lay
As evidence

Distant memories the only marking
Of what was

The past no longer has a pull
Influence or bearing

It has been burned down
Obliterated

My heart can move forward
Finally in gratitude

My being is free
To fulfill its destiny

Not because it was meant to be
Because it's what I chose for me

# Smoke

Every time I need a re-set

Like when I move in

Want to get rid of the past

Wash away density and negativity

I burn sage

Smoke palo santo

Smudge incense

Dropping the ash

Allowing the smoke to fill

And then to clear away

# Hair

A dead protein
Expelled from the body

Cut it
It won't affect

Health or life
Except image

Identity
Expression

Which are vital
To living

Hair is dead
But so much a part

Of who we are
When we're alive

# Hair tie

I keep hair out of my face

It helps me concentrate

Wrap it in a bun

Perhaps a bit too tight

My scalp grows sore

From the tug

The ache spreads

To the rest of my head

Even after I release it

An NSAID is all I've got

Because I haven't yet relaxed

Felt ease and calm

And I may not

Until I let my hair

Hang free

# Hot cup

Waking up to watch

The twilight take shape

Darkness seeping away

From the view through my window

I cherish the few silent moments

To read and write

In peace and quiet

I indulge in the delectable

Quick nourishment of delights

As I embrace a delicious hot cup

Milking up to the last drop

Already looking forward

To it happening

All over again

Tomorrow

# Energy

Inner body

Ener-body

Energy body

Full body

Body full

Feeling body

Inner soul

Ener-soul

Energy soul

Full soul

Soul full

Feeling soul


Inner spirit

Ener-spirit

Energy spirit

Full spirit

Spirit full

Feeling spirit

# Roller coaster

Life is like a roller coaster
Slow times followed by fast ones
And back again

Sometimes we're left hanging
Upside down
And right side up

Unexpectedly, we drop
In exhilarating free-fall
Screaming our heads off

Sometimes we swerve
Fast on a curve
Our insides held together by centrifuge

We rise up
Slowly and with effort
Happily taking deep breaths

And fall
So quick we think we may drop
With our hearts in our throats

But the truth is
We are secure and safe
Strapped in

When the ride ends
Despite the soul-catching moments
We're elated with adrenaline

We realize in this journey
That even the lowest points
Were worth the ride

# Sand timer

My life felt like someone had
Tipped over the hourglass
It spun out of control
Finally stopping to collect sand
In a place it had never been before

I needed to be turned on my head
See things differently
Recognize what I hadn't seen before
Listen to the echoes of words
Advice I had ignored

I heard the warnings
Yet held on to my obstinate blindness
Time passed but it's no matter
It brought a deeper understanding
It was worthwhile to lose my grip

In a roundabout way
It brought stability
A sense of safety and grounding
The illusion ended
I woke up to reality

I finally heard what I'd been told
Time and time before
I needed experience to pass
To learn my lesson
And grow even more

Time may seem like it's up
But with another tip
A turn of the glass
It restarts
Providing another chance

# Dominoes

Life is a series of tumbles
One after another
A perfect synchronicity
Of trips and falls

Without the fall
I wouldn't have developed my stupidity
Without my stupidity
I wouldn't have created my fallacy
Without my fallacy
I wouldn't have bred it into my lunacy
Without my lunacy
I wouldn't have built my delusion
Without my delusion
I wouldn't have carried my misbelief
Without my misbelief
I wouldn't have followed my blind spot

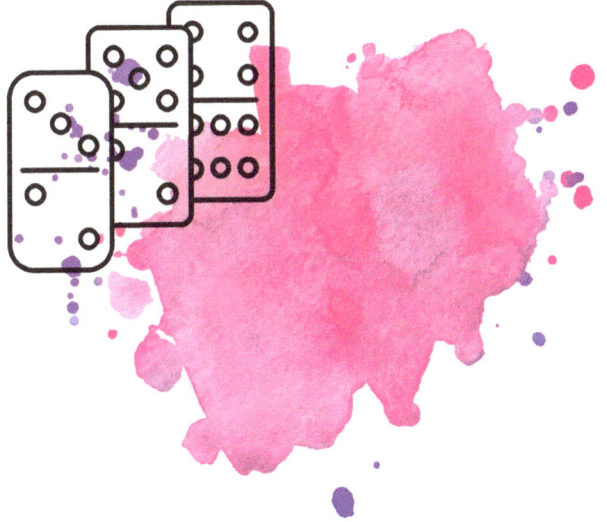

Without my blind spot

I wouldn't have gathered my courage

Without my courage

I wouldn't have pursued my dreams

Without my dreams

I wouldn't have realized my mistake

Without my mistake

I wouldn't have accepted my fall


Falling into place

Life is a series of decisions

Taking us from one spot to another

In perfect synchronicity

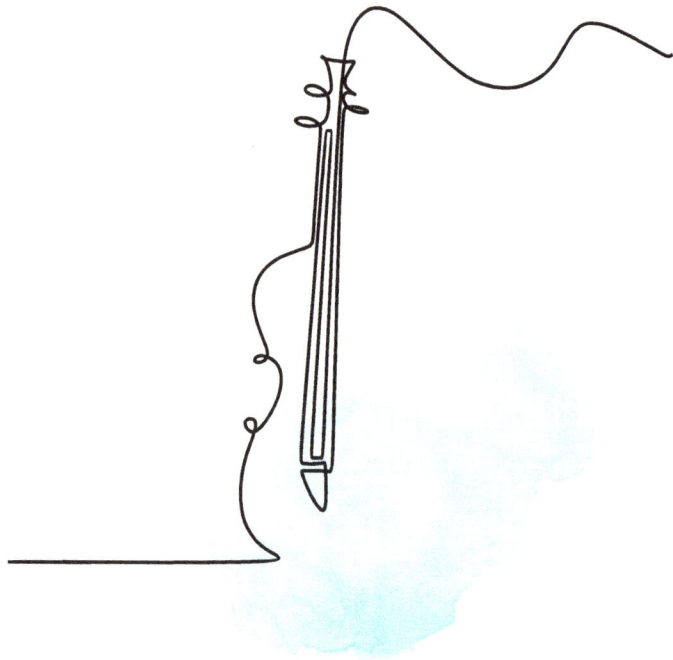

# Strings

The next song plays

Strings strum deep melodies

Nasal vocals pull at my heart

For a time and place

Where nostalgia struck

When there was

Less to prove and less to pursue

Not succumbing to flashy tunes

Simplicity through and through

Honored our fold

Conjured our lore

Not feeling the need to chase

The type of music

That wakens the soul

# Flutes

A woman plays a wooden flute

She has many

In boxwood, cedar, cocobolo, and mopani


She plays twice a day

At least

A unique frequency rolls out of her


She emits healing tunes

Wakens the senses with ancient lore

Her melodies take us on journeys


Like an eagle soaring through the sky

A deep spiritual perspective

Keen eye and a unique vision

Like a turtle that swims in solitary calmness

Self-sufficient in the vast ocean

Carrying its home for its eternal longevity


Sage collected in their travels

The eagle and turtle intersect in the flute

A rare happenstance of shared wisdom


When the woman plays

Air, wood, and water combine with a fiery passion

The elements join forces to share tales


A dense canopy in the Catskills

Moving zig-zag around tree trunks

Slow paced with a sense of calm and peace

People wearing thick wool ponchos

Looking down on the ruins of a village

From the top of the Andean mountains


A gust blowing that flops the hair

While standing on a mesa

In the Arizona red rock


Blue skies above

While water trickles down a soft cascade

As a river makes its way through Alaska


The ocean reveals a gentle ebb and flow

With a light soothing breeze through the Keys

As the sun shines in soft light


Open ears receive the healing

Without ever having to hear

All because of a woman


Who plays her soulful melodies

Where eagles and turtles meet

Through hand-carved wooden flutes

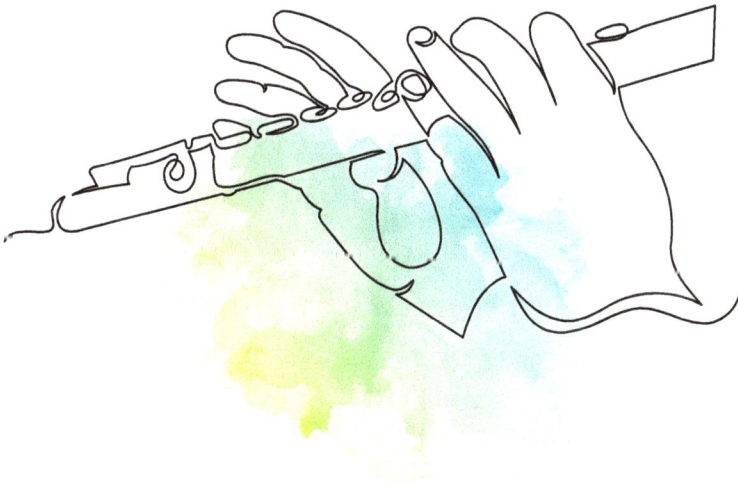

# Nature

Animal spirits, elements, fauna, flora, weather

# Green thumbs

I didn't grow up with green thumbs

A shame I would say

For the botanist and agriculturist

Who raised me

No plant I could keep alive

Until I named it


What a wonder it was

To give a living thing a life

A personality to connect with

That made all the difference

For genes to ignite

My care for nature

Now I wonder how for so long

I missed out on marvels

Creations best displays

Of evolution's survival

The most well adapted

To me and mine

# Spore

Delicate yet filled with might
They spur throwing caution to the wind
Careening into the world
Twisting and turning in merriment

Until they drop to the ground
The earth folds them in a cocoon of warmth
Until they are invigorated by wetness
To draw on its resources

Germinating the nourishment
In a transformative explosion
That begins beyond the reaches of the eye
Until the piercing moment

The ground breaks open
Revealing the momentous greenness

I wonder

If the spore fulfills its dreams

If it releases gleeful exclamations

As it twirls in the air


Feeling freedom

And surrender

As it is carried away

Every which way


I wonder how it decides

When and where to drop

Or if it trusts the universe

Knowing it has been placed


Exactly where it needs to be

To fulfill its purpose


I wonder if it dreams

Of how high

And how green

It will grow

Sprouting out from the mounds
Of the earth that nestled it
Until conditions
Were just so

I wonder if I too
Can be so fancy-free

Trusting I have
What I need
To fulfill
What I am here to give

I wonder too if I can
Surrender my dreams
Trusting the universe
Will deliver me in the right conditions

And so we must too
Draw out our seeds

Allow them to twist and turn

Holding their unfolding potential

Until they get the exact conditions

They need to nourish and germinate


Tend to them with thought and care

Bursting into brightness

So they may grow

Into the might they hold

# Winds

Change is in the air

A breeze sweeps through

Gentle and nudging

The newness rocks me

Into relaxation

Caressing me into a lull

Making it essential

For the gust that follows

Blowing into disarray

Rocking me into awareness

Alert and on guard

To be confident

I will have to seek

For my own path

With the same determination

Relentlessly pushing ahead

Leaving the calm winds behind

# Cliff

I have always wished

To have a house

High up on a cliff

Overlooking the crashing waves

Almost able to touch the clouds

As if hoisted on wings

Watching the delectable pass

Nourishing my kin

With burning fires within

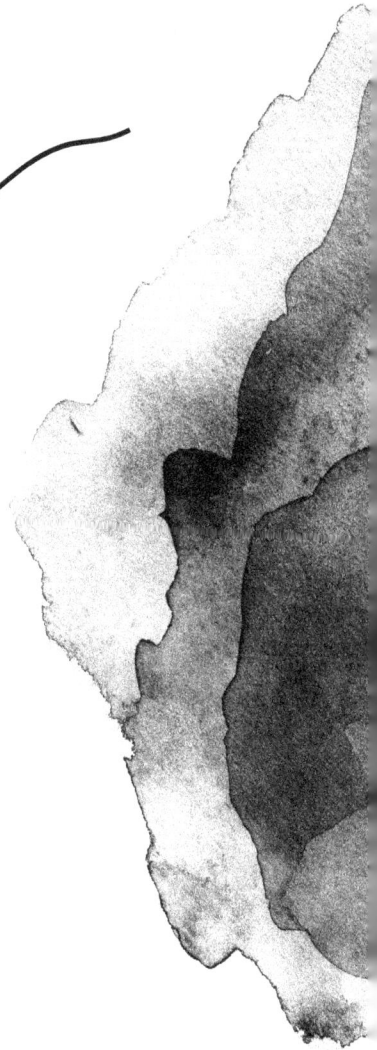

# Water

Nourishing
A source
Building life
70% of us all
We thrive and survive

Providing
Abundantly flowing
With ease
From one place to the next
Always shifting yet present

Breaking
Boulders chiseled
Persistent and patient
Against whatever stands in its way
Sometimes pounding and grinding

Moving

Without concern

Focused intently

On where it must go

Never tiring or pausing


Carving

Its path

Following its purpose

Like I wish I could

Had I strength and courage

# Ocean

Healing water beckons

Plunging into her warmth

Saltiness seeps into my pores

A mermaid once called mythical

Finally at home

# The beach

Beads glisten in the light
It's barely been a minute
Toasting under the sun

Wish for cool and shade
Despite love for radiance
Brown skin must not burn

Sea oats sway over dunes
Mindful of loggerhead nests
Gentle taunt of the breeze

Tote and flip flops anchor
Plop in a dreadful mess
Cradle bent knees

Retriever splashes over tennis ball

Horseshoe crab tumbles in waves

Dolphin pod dives in delight


Hues change in the expanse

Pale greens and deep blues

Shiver at the enormity


Trepidation met with grittiness

Release the cords

Surrender to the sirens

# Noseeums

I often get inspiration
In the strangest of places
And less often
In the most expected of places

The ocean is a continuous stream
Of healing and renewal
A certain source of inspiration
I knew it would be for me that day

I watched the ebb and flow of waves
The endless blue of the horizon
Wondering how a blue could be so dark
So deep

I closed my eyes

Willing inspiration to hit

I needed it

Things hadn't been working out for me


I couldn't wait for circumstances to shift

Pain and bliss come and go

I knew the sadness would soon fade

Even the good soon dissipates


It should make it easier

During tough moments

Because they too

Will pass


It should also make it easier

To appreciate the good times

Because they too

Will pass

Suddenly
I felt pricks on my arms
Oh no, I thought
It can't be

The sensation reminded me
Of those nasty noseeums
Nature's antique weapon
Against disbelief and doubt

Clearly, I needed more faith
It was useless to will my way against fate
I wouldn't get what I wanted
Only what I needed

# Dove

It persists daily

The image, bird, and word

Flashing all around me

Same family as a pigeon

In more colors than just white

An emblematic symbol

Of peace and of love

The purity of friendship

Handling challenges with ease

The message repeatedly appears

To release the past

Embrace hope and salvation

A dignifying harmony

Linking my thoughts

With my reality

# Hawk

Hawks represent focus and strength
Open to awareness

This morning one perched
In my backyard on a tree

To offer a broader perspective
Spiritual insight

It's never been here before
It was small and searching

A wintery hunt
Repeatedly attempting

To freely roam the skies
Use a discerning eye

To catch
A smaller winged prey

Make use of your resources
Trust your instinct

# Owl

It's the animal spirit
Of one of my dear ones
I used to see one
On my daily rounds
Of The Battery

The bird of wisdom
Often depicted with glasses
Despite their impeccable vision
And ability to see beyond
What the light shines upon

Trust the mystery
Listen to your intuition
Allow your head to twist
So that you can see
What others can't

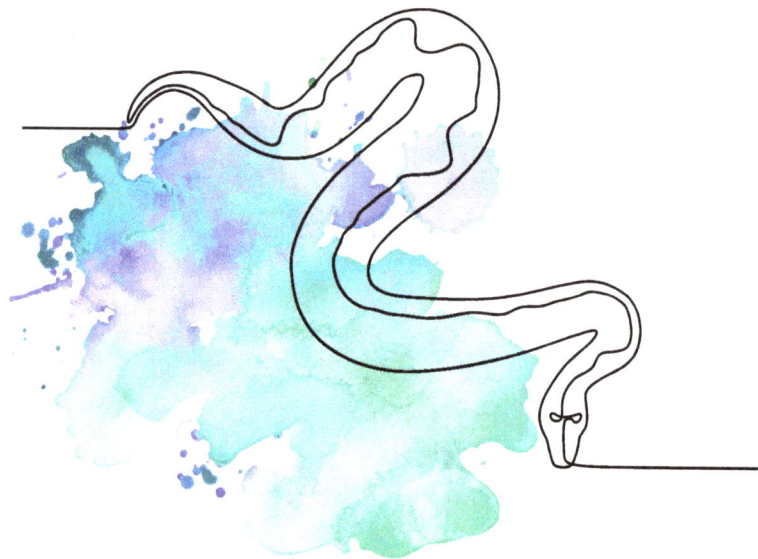

# Snake

Signals transformation

Shedding of baggage

Released to make space

Igniting the life force within

A healing that transmutes

What's no longer needed

# Monkey

With skillful light-heartedness

They gather in temples

Reining in strength and courage

Of our dear Hanuman

Our inquisitive consciousness

Mischievously grabbing

Sickly sugary parshad

A monkey mind unsettled

Until the prize is in hand

Joyfully bringing levity

To an otherwise solemn event

In that way the monkey

Processes empathy and understanding

Sharing our beloved indulgences

Showing us that with intelligence

Smart eyes

Quick hands

And plenty of wit

We too can steal away

Sweet boxes

Of delight

# Night

My favorite part of the day
When the time comes to wind down
And snuggle into
How we spend half of our lives
Sleep

As quiet and stillness settle
The time to recuperate and restore
Filling us with energy to begin again
Darkness envelopes
Night

# Day

Heating water and milk

Lead to soul warming

Spicy gingery tea

Sipped in between bites

Of a cashew pistachio chew


A few pages of reading

Lead to soul warming

Along with at least three

Pages of handwritten things

So my mind has less on to chew

A few yoga poses

Lead to soul warming

So that my mornings allow

My body to get ready

To chew what comes next


Finally a few minutes of strength

Lead to soul warming

Hot steam with energizing oils

Setting me up

To chew on this day of delight

# Moon phases

Every 30 days or so
Our lady of the night
Waxes and then wanes

New for beginning
Fresh starts and creativity
Manifesting intentions

Full for completion
Closing and resetting
Releasing to make space

Every month another cycle
Presents a fresh set of opportunities
To start and re-set

# Earthquake

The ground shakes

The earth growls

Sputters and quakes

Letting us know

In the heart of it all

It's pulsing and growing

More in control of us

Than we care to admit

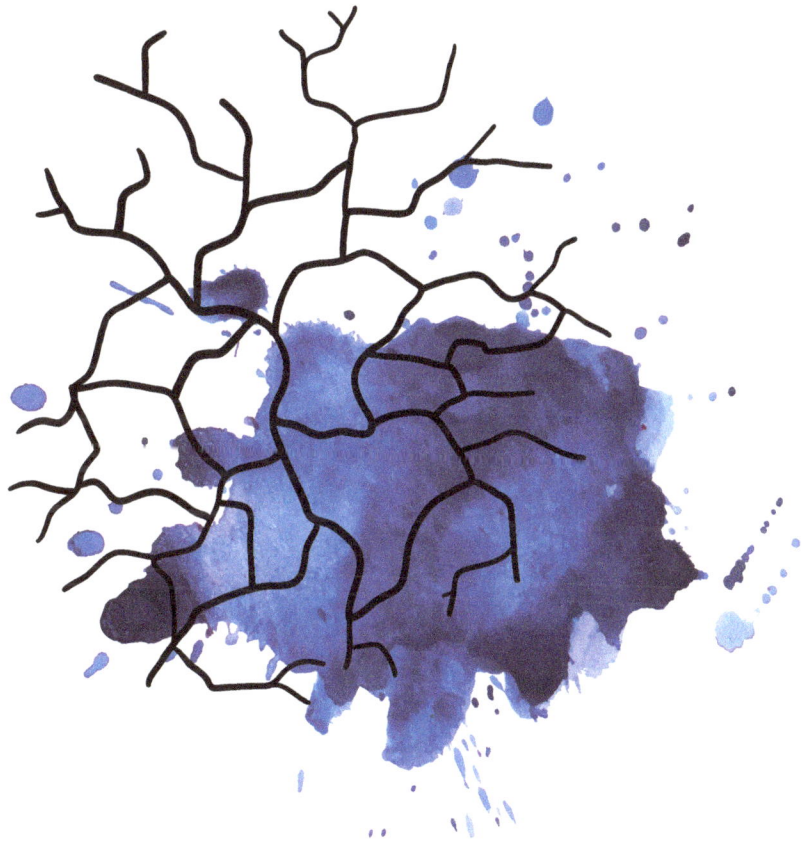

# Seasons

Seasons come
And they go

Marking the passing of time

Where I grew up
It wasn't so

Only two

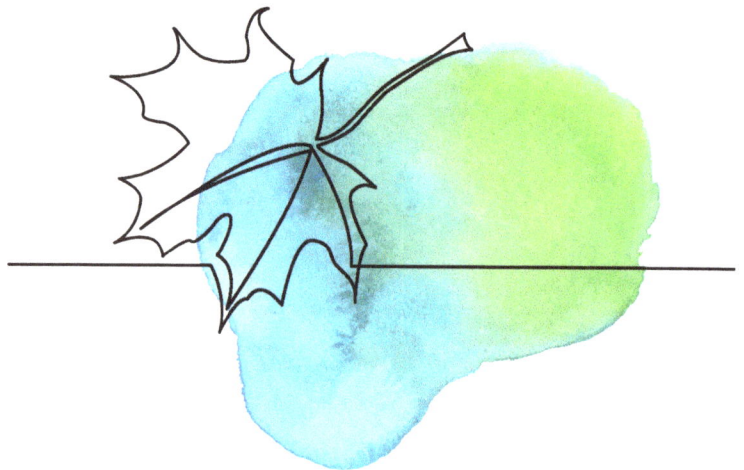

One hot
The other rainy

Where I live
It's markedly so

Winter dies
Spring is born
Summer renews
Fall detoxes

Seasons come
And they go

Marking the passing of time

# Sunset

My eyes set on the horizon

Emerging hues on their daily voyage

Through the skies

Picking up the pure wisdom of white

Dazzling yellows with golden eternal awareness

Redness tracks progress in our hearts

A push and pull of love and wrath

A brief pause in vital orange

Cool blues hint of their sentimental clues

A longing for what's ending

The lushness of the green day

A distant recollection

The darkness rises

Drawing us into the unknown

Where we have no choice but to rely

On our inner guidance

To set the course

Of this thing

We call life

# Solstice

Solstice is a special time

Electricity charges the skies

Pouring down into our beings

Whether we are connected or not

On the darkest night

And the lightest day

How can it be

Any other way

It's the dead of winter

Or the heat of summer

We're cuddled up in padding

Or skipping in bikinis

We're layered in blankets

Or in sunscreen

We're slurping hot lamb stew

Or a lime popsicle

The in-between
Comes on other days
That are no less magical
But less obviously so
Solstice is a special time

Axial path of the sun in alignment
Blooming away from the distant
Celestial Equator
December it comes
Equinox it's not

Focus on the sun
Gradually reaching
Heightened energies
Incidental moments
June it comes again

Kwanzaa is celebrated
Longest night but not the longest day
Midsummer not midwinter
Navigation for many on earth

Orbiting around the sun

Paths we follow

Quests fulfilled

Rotating prograde to create

Shortest day and longest night


Terminators divide day and night over the Tropics

Uniquely at

Vertex

Winter begins

Xeric summer comes

Yester time released and future embraced

Zodiacs affected

# Numbers

Count, digits, measure, numerals, value

# Dualities

Living a life of illusion
Symbolic and opposite

Sun and moon
Rise and fall

Present in every aspect
Truth and lies

Inertia and liveliness
Weighty and subtle

In our lives
Pleasure and pain

Tailbone and skull
Blood and breath

The energies
Push and pull

Depth and surface
Dormant and brilliant

The weather
Clouds and sun

Stagnation and transformation
Asleep and awake

How we grow
Spiritual and grounded

Quiescence and bubbliness
Boundless and constricted

The choices we make
Black and white

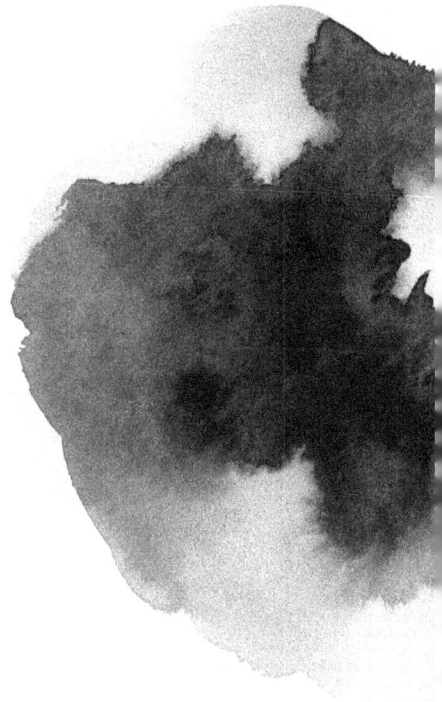

Cane and ladder
Front and back

What we feel
Ebb and flow

Tingle and dullness
Fear and courage

The marking of time
Night and day

Genesis and conclusion
Pilgrimage and hibernation

Reduced to two
Masculine and feminine

Attune and conflict
Aberration and sanity

As if we can be reduced
One and two

Win and lose
Active and passive

What really matters
Smiling and frowning

Hate and love
Doubt and confidence

Is existence
Zero and one

Skepticism and hope
Having and lacking

What we learn
Anger and joy

Sadness and bliss

Pride and forgiveness

Make sure we are whole

Hot and cold

Yin and yang

Happiness and despair

So many others

Give and take

Heaven and hell

Open and close

It's hard to keep track

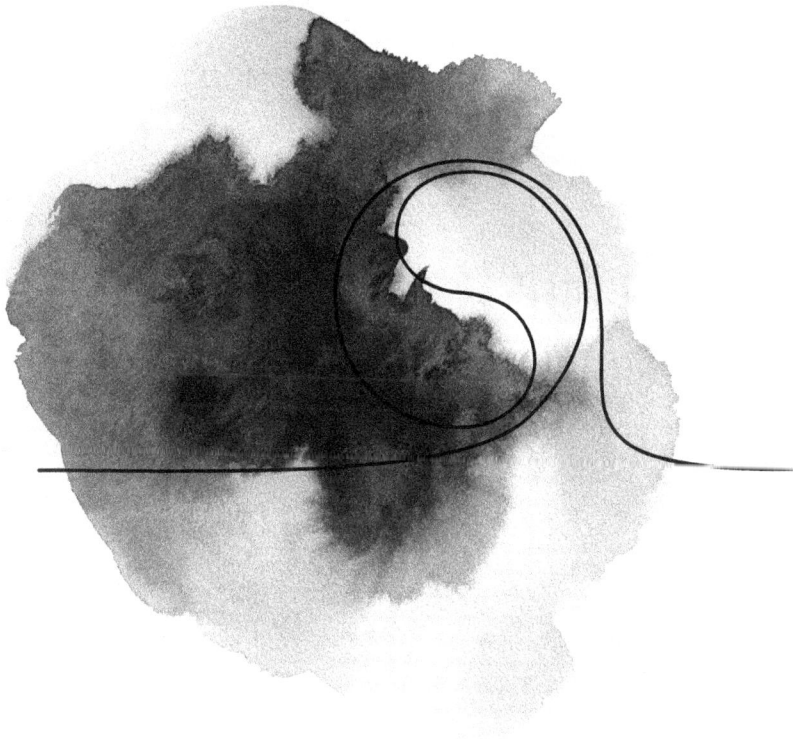

# Three things

For a few years now
I have tried to keep
To just three things

A magic number it seems
In my daily to-do
It is the key to de-stress

I used to fill
My task list to the brim
I didn't know how to begin

Now I am satisfied with just three
Ironically freeing my time
To do many more things

# Threes

Matter plant animal
Inanimate living conscious
Live die regenerate

Ebb pause flow
Inhale pause exhale
Exhale pause inhale

Repose silence peace
Suffer learn live
Believe surrender be

# Four words

Change self-care magic purpose
Four words meant to

Describe the themes
For the new phase

Change is quiet stillness
Listen to inner guidance

Self-care is opening
Feelings flood in

Magic creates connection
With all there is

Purpose is allowing freedom
Be our true selves

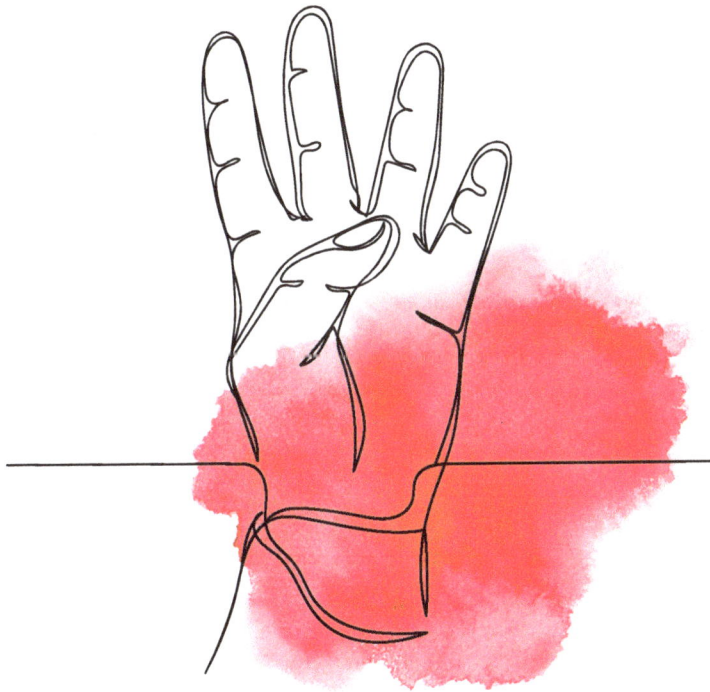

# Another four

Gratitude strength breakthrough lesson

Appreciation for all I have

Stand confident in who I am

Achieving a life of purpose

Having overcome personal challenges

What a beautiful life lesson


Based on a puzzle

A grid filled with letters

The first four show

The theme for the future

As if life were

Just a crossword puzzle

I play anyway

Four more words appear

That give motivation

And a bit of inspiration

Of what is possible to create

What's the harm anyway


This particular puzzle

Another set of words

An innocent game

Brought about unexpected wisdom

Depth and meaning

From a mere puzzle

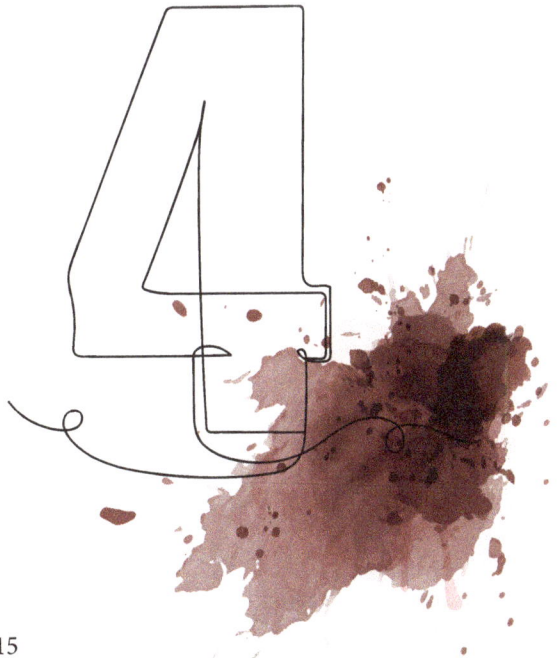

# Five

2021 adds up to five

Change and transformation

Not in a vacuum

Open up to evolution

Claim personal power

Take action

Create the circumstances


I claim responsibility

Finally accepting

I come first

Fit your oxygen mask

Then place one on others

That is my action

My change

# Seven

Days in a week
Colors of the rainbow
Chakras in the body
Deadly sins
Magdalene's wraths
Sages

Lucky number
That of my path
An assurance
Headed in the right direction
Wisdom and knowledge
Seeker

Depth and meaning

Find purpose

If seven is my number

Does that mean I have my purpose

Or I'll spend my life

Seeking

# Seven areas

Embrace love

Love myself

Trust the universe

Trust myself

Release the struggle

Feel joy

I am here now

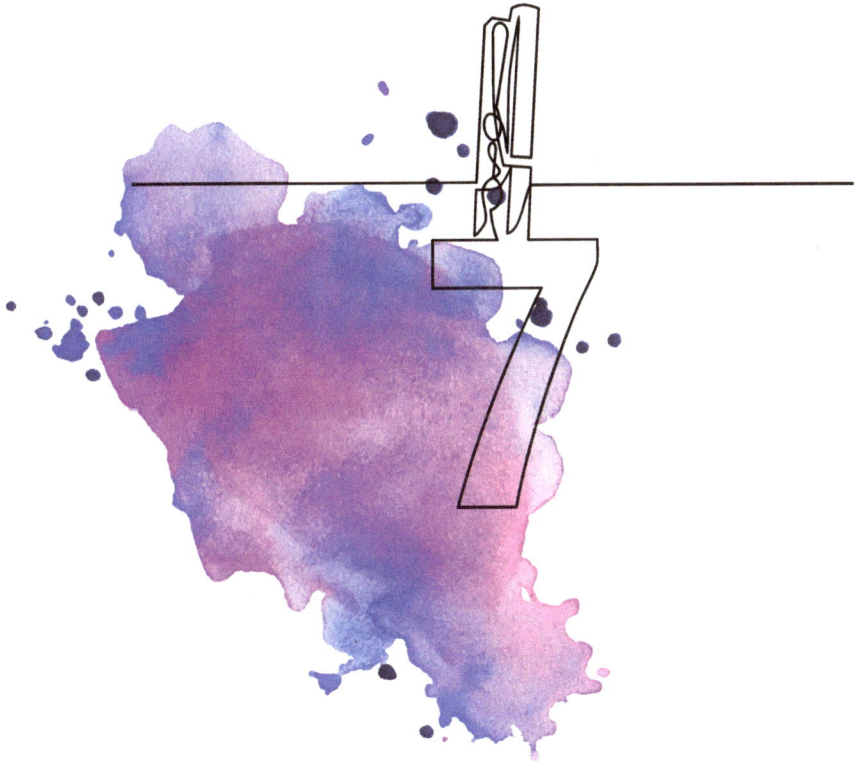

# Eight

The lemniscate

An infinity turned up

Or is infinity

An eight turned horizontal

Signifying life is but a cycle

Of ending and beginnings

One flowing into another

An endless turning

Of life and death

When one cycle ends

Another begins

Repetitive vitality

Occurring infinitely

# Twelve

A master number

Like eleven

Doesn't add to three

Strong energy

When you see it

It's a message

Step out of what's comfortable

Take that leap

Trust what's coming

Positive is on its way

Ascension is unfolding

Reach for your highest potential

Get rid of negativity

Be confident

Allow for personal growth

Open up to success

Set intentions

Then take a step back

And watch it all unfold

# Thirty-three

Be

Be authentic

Be in love with yourself

Be in the flow

Be loved

Be ONE

Be who you are, unapologetically

unabashedly

Believe

Calm

Connect to source

Deserve

Expand

Feel abundant

Feel compassion

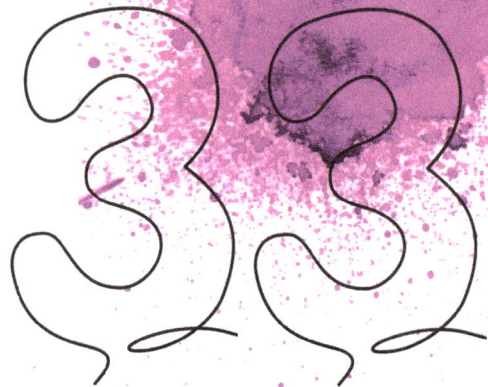

Feel worthy

Follow inner guidance

Forgive

Grow, always

Have unwavering faith

Learn

Live life

Love

Maintain healthy boundaries

Make deep connections

Pursue health

Read, avidly

Recognize your value

Speak truth

Surround by love

Touch the lives of many

Travel

Trust in magic

Unfold amazingly

# 108

One zero and eight
A sacred number
Together as 108
Ultimate

Right side up
And down
The numbers look the same
Resonance

The line is the one
A form of infinity
It links one to another
Connection

# 108

The plane is the zero
An object
No end and no beginning
Cycle

The solid is the eight
A loop
Infinity turned to its side
Unity

Together they represent
A progression into light
Compassion and tolerance
Wholeness

# 240 colored pens

My hand glides with ease

With every imaginable color

I haven't run out in a year


Building a new arc in the rainbow

Every ten pages or less

Gaia hates the plastic wastage


Neons blind me in the dark

Darks that bleed into the other side

Shades so light I can't read my writing

Glitter explodes in addition

Colorful dimensions enhance my life

Stuck to me for days


Gels of inspiration

For records, sayings, and musings

Innovation creates wonders

# 2,668,727

How is it possible

To reach 2,668,727

And people not believe

The severity of this disease


How is it possible

To reach 2,668,727

And people not believe

The important of mask-wearing

Social-distancing and other safety measures


How is it possible

To reach 2,668,727

And people not believe

They are being selfish

That what they do makes a difference

Their actions affect others

How is it possible

To reach 2,668,727

And people not believe

The cruelty of the situation

The severity of the death

That it's several million

Compassion makes all the difference


Only because it is possible

For more than 2,668,727

Souls to pass on

To another dimension

Do we acknowledge their time

Love and contribution

During their years on earth

Take a moment to honor them

# Coincidence

I see the same numbers
In several different places
Is that a coincidence

There is no such thing
Everything happens precisely
As it is meant to be

In perfect synchronicity
Paths crossing
At the exact time and place

Repeating numbers
11:11, 12:34, 5:55
Signs I notice

Energies rising
Pointing a direction
Nudging to evolve

Because that is how it is meant
Choices that led us here
The reason is yet to be determined

I get the clues
When I'm paying attention
When I need to know

These are no coincidences
Only messages from above
In beautiful synchronicity

# Palindrome

Same forward as backward

A unique reflection

As above so within

As without so below

Pay attention to signs and signals

Dreams and messages

The divine entourage

Communicating

We are mere reflections

Of something bigger and grander


2021 started with a series

The American way

12021, 12121, 12221, 12321, 12421, 12521, 12621,

12721, 12821, 12921

Converging with the Lunar New Year

New Moon energy reigned

Opening a window

Genuine love and generosity

Growing into a clear horizon

Where calm is palpable

There is ease in the being


Today is another palindrome

If you look at the date

The non-American way

The rest of the world way

12022021

A sign of true alignment

Will for co-creating

With the universe

Supporting us

As it always does

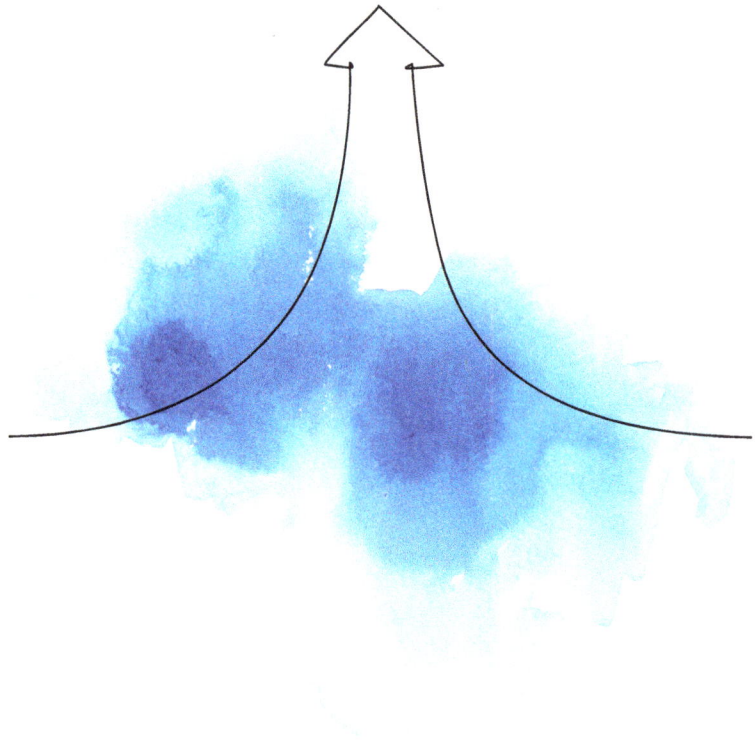

# Rising

It is no coincidence

That Kamala was introduced

On 12021 at 11:11

And Amanda was reciting

Awe inspiring poetry at 12:21

A sign of the changes

In the right direction

An elevation

Women rise

An energetic elevation

That's what palindromes mean

And Angelic numbers

A promise for better

A shift that new times are here

That this time is ours

# 2021

Today is the first day

The start of a new year

We left 2020

It's in hindsight

Seems an ordinary

Friday

The air feels different

My spirit takes in more

Sensing the possibility

Unfettered exploration

Places to go

Seek

Next time I see you

My arms will wrap

Tight like a bear

Regardless of how much

Or little your

Regard


Such a simple act

Yet so markedly novel

Given what we just left

It's a new year

A time to begin

Again

# Chinese New Year

If I looked at the calendar
I would be a wise snake
According to the lunar ticks
It makes me a grand dragon

Begins on 212 with determined metal
2021 year of the self-assured Ox
Between the new and full moon
Days of sheep-like harmonious celebration

Shine like the role model rooster
Distributing lycee red packets
With the generosity of a rabbit
For luck and abundance

Set out fish and oranges
Emitting charisma like a monkey
Witty and cute like the rabbit
Or like a warm-hearted pig

Time to do a deep cleanse
Gather friends and family
With the faithful friendliness of a dog
And the open-minded gait of a horse

Kung hei fat choi
Culminating with lanterns
Set intentions for what's coming
With a keen eye of the tiger

# One year

I started the year
Feeling trapped

Then I moved on to hurt
But with friendship I healed

Mixed in I also felt loved
Purpose came and set course

The right direction it seemed
Until the jitters of lockdown

At first I felt I would thrive
And in a way I did

But it also broke me
I sunk further still

What ensued were quarrels
Battles within and without

I managed to construct a silo
Who would have thought

Disconnection was possible
During a quarantine

Wasn't I disconnected
Enough already

I shattered my surroundings
Feeling oppressed

Broke the silo
Forged new connections

But the struggles ensued
Didn't end

Yet I persisted
Facing no other choice

Somehow amidst the frustration
The shell cracked

I found myself
Again

Except I was no longer
Who I used to be

I was still me
With a few more white hairs

A few burns
And scratches

I was
A different me

Perhaps I had released
What was trapped

It had to crack and break

Let go of the shell

Expose new flesh

And emerge afresh

In this new year

I woke to realize

I had grown and transmuted

Pain into healing

The shift was palpable

I felt hope

# Practices & Beliefs

Divine, faith, mystical, rituals, spiritual

# Birth day

The day of our birth
A celebration of who we are

A testament we are on this earth
For one more spin around the sun

Hurt when not acknowledged
Touched when someone does

Makes us feel we matter
The only time we don't question it

We are here for a reason
With a purpose

Maybe the time I question it the most
Wondering why I have come

What pulled me to incarnate
Am I doing what I came to do

How big do my actions have to be
To matter

How small must my ego be
To not stand in the way

How much of a footprint must I leave (or not)
How tenderly must I step

Do I damage or improve
Do I do both

Does it matter
Do I matter

Why else would I be here
What else would I do

Be myself and be the best version of me
That is all

The only reason we are called
To this earth

We are the only ones who question
When we get quiet and still

Focus only on the present moment
We realize we lack for nothing

Doing what we are meant to be doing
No matter how big or small

Whatever action we take
Is just right

Knowing we are who we are meant to be
When we begin another year of existence

# Diwali

A festive occasion

Brightens our lives

With love and joy

A celebration

Of all that is good

Knowledge illuminating

Our inner truth

Sparking the flames

Of the light

We hold within

# Breathing

Thank you for being with me

In every moment of my existence

Infusing love in every breath

Allowing me to receive in every inhale

Spread it with every exhale

Allowing me to be an active participant

In every pulse of the universe

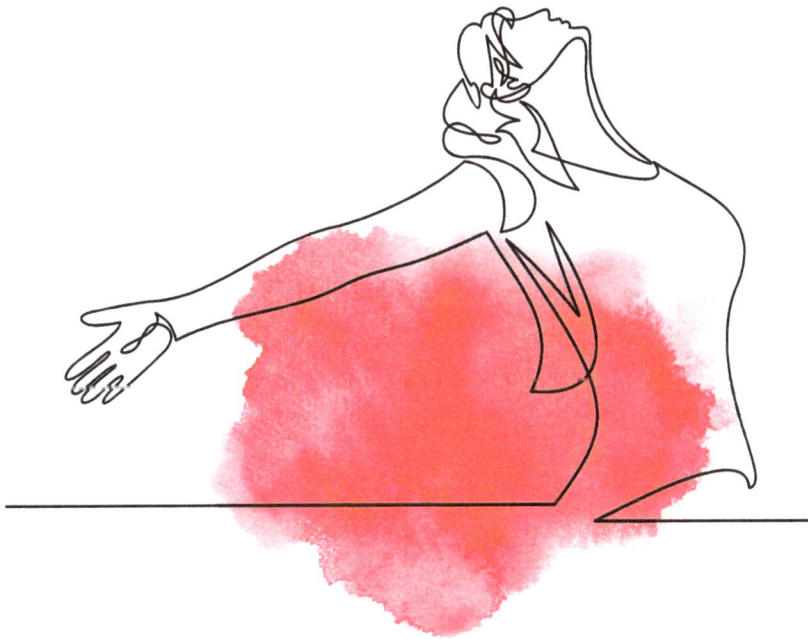

# Thought

I need only watch

A ticking time bomb

I watch it try

Run what I feel

No, what I think

Then what I feel

It's my decision

Allow it to take hold

To indulge

Grasp its poisonous tentacles

Sink in its venomous fangs

I can't stop it

Its murkiness seeps through my veins

It invades me

Takes flight in my being

The turbulence rises

Pressure cooker heightens

In my mind

Something clicks

A sudden realization

A whistle blowing me into alertness

Wait a minute

This isn't how it has to be

It's my choice

I am the one

Who can stop it

Gently release the steam

Letting it escape

Settle down and cool off

Quiet the world

Allow calmness to take hold

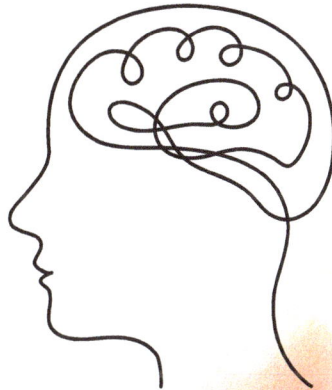

# Contemplation

Studying a thought or feeling

As if it were a researchable topic

Becoming more knowledgeable

With aspects of ourselves

Our actions and behaviors

Have we always experienced this

It too will come to an end

What do we want to feel

Why is that so meaningful

What is the reality

What can we do about it

What can we let go

And so we ponder

Becoming more knowledgeable

With aspects of ourselves

Our actions and behaviors

Contemplating who we are

# Samadhi

First heard it on a Live song

In my college years

Sang along not knowing

Took me years to learn

It's a meditative state

Of calm and insight

A tranquil consciousness

That leads to wisdom

Clearing the mind

To bring in sharpness

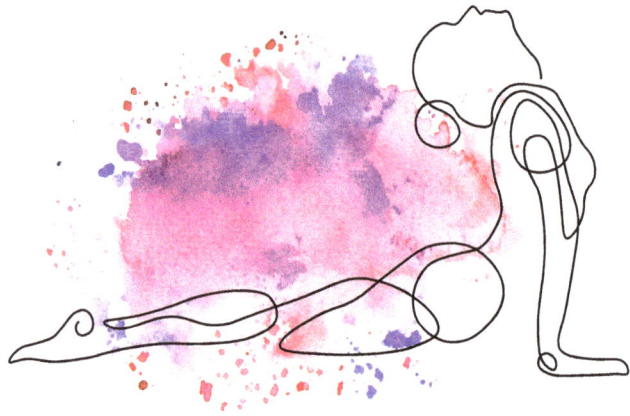

# Movement

I first signed

21 days to a habit

Connect the yang of the skull with the yin of the tail

Stand to waken the soles of the head

Pull on the mind of the feet

Extract nectar from the webbed taproot

Build a resilient fascia support

Trampoline into twists and bends

Stable bridges of lift

Strike in the heel that doesn't clench the buttocks

Lift in the quads pumps foundation to the lungs

Distortion in the feet doesn't clog emotions

Spring in the diaphragm gives resilience to the organs

Savasana to drop into the ground

Allowing a full bloom of the temple

Gradually increasing the mark

I upped the ante

365 days of movement

# Mantra

The Gayatri Mantra
I should have learned
Sanskrit words
To be guided by light
I didn't study Hinduism
Instead I learned

The Padre Nuestro
Hallowed be thy name
Que se haga tu voluntad
A universal message readily repeated
But I didn't study Catholicism
Although in one such country I grew

In the next I heard so often

The Serenity Prayer

Linked to AA that I didn't attend

Knowing the difference

And having the wisdom

I still hoped for

And so I attempted

My own repetition

To calm my crazily active mind

In some type of meditation

I am exactly

As I am meant to be

# Dreams

Visions of possibility
Yet we limit them
Making them unrealistic
Or thinking they are

That is the heart
Of the limitation
How can dreams come true
If deep within we don't believe

It's not possible
It can't come together
We don't have time
It's too late

Because we didn't find the strength
Courage, energy, or motivation
Something else was more important
Someone else more deserving

Another more worthy
Than what we wanted
Too inconceivable or unlikely
Because we were not enough

Not good, talented, beautiful, attractive
Simply not enough
Enough
Some one or thing led us to believe

But we have all
What we need
If only we open our inner eyes
To see we can accomplish

Draw forth
The light we hold inside
See that everything is possible
Dreams do come into reality

# Dream world

I have recently had

Such strange dreams

I can't seem to explain

Distinguishing is hard

What is coming

Is it a sign

Is it a vision

Did I create it

Out of imagination

Or did you send it

Led by the divine

The two mix together

And I can't tell

What is made up

What is a message

What is a sign

What my brain is processing

What I am guiding

What is guiding me

I don't know what to make of it

Is it something

Or nothing

I simply let go

Trying to control

What I see

Making sense of it all

Trying to decipher

I want to see

What will come

I want to know

But maybe I don't

Maybe I shouldn't

Then where is it

The charm is within

In the unknown

The unexpected

The surprise

It can blow your mind

Make your heart explore

Because it is better

Than what you imagined

Better than

What came to you

In those strange dreams

# Sacrifice

How do I know
What to believe
Do I have one
Or do I not

In the deepest part
I know I have one
It's a trend
I know

But also a truth

In search I am

I sacrifice

Toss caution


Take chances

Gamble with my future

Treading with certainty

With the knowledge


I set forth

Knowing this effort

Will yield

Union

# Ignorance

Not knowing
Knowing a falsehood
Not discerning the difference
Ignorance

Falling
Getting up again
Struggling to make ends meet
Not ignorance

Cult-like behavior
Failing at trying
Making ourselves seem small
Ignorance

Accepting everyone
And everything for what it is
Infusing life with light
Not ignorance

Thinking one life matters more than another

Judgment and criticism

Putting another down

Ignorance


Making the best of what you've got

Kindness and compassion

Generosity in deed and spirit

Not ignorance


Making ourselves better

Making others bigger

Making other smaller

Ignorance


Our connection to everything and everyone

The eternity of our souls

Our part in oneness

Not ignorance

# Truth

I am not complete
We are not whole
Unless with that someone
Without whom we don't exist
That is not truth

I am separate from you
We don't need anyone
We can survive alone
We are separate from others
That is not truth

I am different than you
We are all different
Differences separate us
Distance makes us different
That is not truth

I am not deserving

We are not worthy

There is a lack

We are defined by this

That is not truth


I am better than you

Yours is better than mine

You are better than me

Any form of comparison

That is not truth


That is not truth


Not truth leads to dislike

Not truth leads to bitterness

Not truth leads to anger


Truth matters

# Cure

The cure for ignorance is compassion

Not anger not hurt not insult

The cure for ignorance is love

Understanding kindness and generosity

The cure for ignorance is truth

# Sharing

Sometimes it's easier to talk to a stranger

Reveal one's secrets

Things we wouldn't share with whom we know

Fearing judgment, criticism, ostracism

Putting us at a disadvantage

Being marginalized or excluded

Thought less of

Liked and loved less


There's a freedom in revealing

The unnamed face knowing

What we won't share

A burden unleashed

A weight removed from our shoulders

Suddenly we move with ease

We have shared a secret

Taken a risk with a stranger

# Passing on

Baby and crone

An intricate relation

Created because of a step in between

One with all the life lived

The master

The other with a life yet to live

The novice

One teaching, mentoring the other

Passing on traditions and rituals

Wisdom only known to those

Who have been

So the other may have less

Wobbly of a walk

Tools to stand up from the stumble

An endless cycle of transmission

Teacher to student

One passes on

So the other lives on

# Existence

Do I cease to exist because the universe ceases

Do I exist because the universe does


Does a drop in the ocean make it

Does the ocean dry because it is missing a drop


Does a tree die because a leaf falls

Does a bird ground because a feather drops


Without all its feathers a bird can't fly

Without all its leaves a tree decays

Without all its drops an ocean wouldn't be

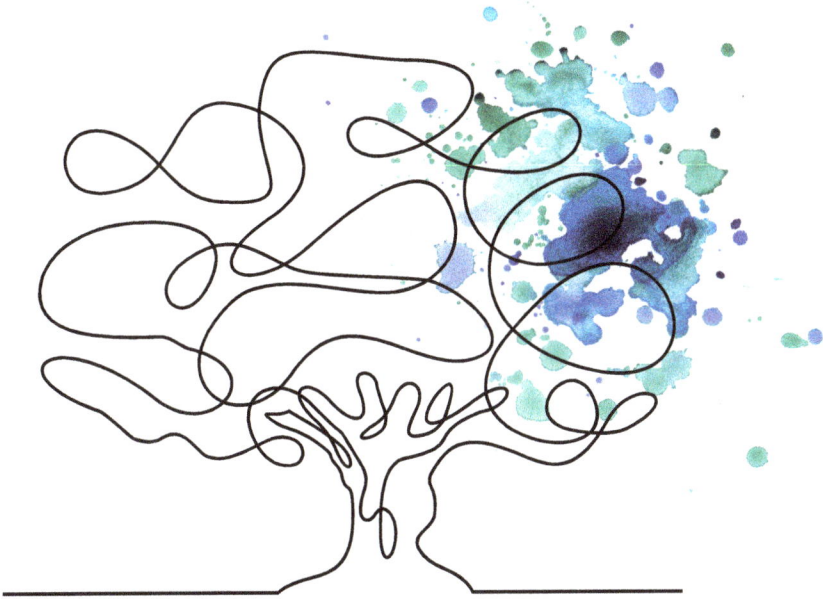

I exist because the universe does

The universe exists because I do


An individual may not matter

The collective does


The collective is made up of individuals

As an individual I do matter

# Soul

If you cease to exist

Your soul doesn't

It comes back in another form

Always part of the whole

# Unique

You are no different

Or more special

Than another

Yet you are special

In your uniqueness

# Tantra

It's not what you think
The term has been used erroneously
It's a link between
Student and teacher

A doctrine or a practice
Leading to liberation
Dialoguing directly with deities
Showing the sacredness in all

Philosophy on life
Connecting movement and physicality
Weaving inner energy and consciousness
Composing action and performance

Breaking free

From ignorance and suffering

Through a direct union

With the divine


Yogic purification

Intertwining destruction and creation

Awakening the kundalini

The serpent rising


Yoga isn't just work on the mat

Yoga is any kind of work or practice

Done with the intention

Of ascendence

# Symbols

Ancient wisdom, emblems, meaning,
representations, signs

# Dot

The simplest of symbols
Encompasses wholeness
Unity
All there is
In simplicity

What we each are
A mere dot
When put together
Each of us
Make up a painting

A kaleidoscope
A mosaic
Of several dots
That make up
The universe

# Magic of words

I think I am pushing now

To be creative by force

Only because I'm determined

I want to produce more

That keeps me moving

As does this pen

Whose ink I'm waiting to run out

So that I can throw it away

And finally move this pad of paper

Back on my desk

I don't know how it's possible

For a series of symbols

Created for language

To carry so much meaning

Expressing what I can't seem to describe

Release what I hold inside

And elicit compassion

Or at least understanding

Or even still

Someone else to listen

To the magic of words

I share

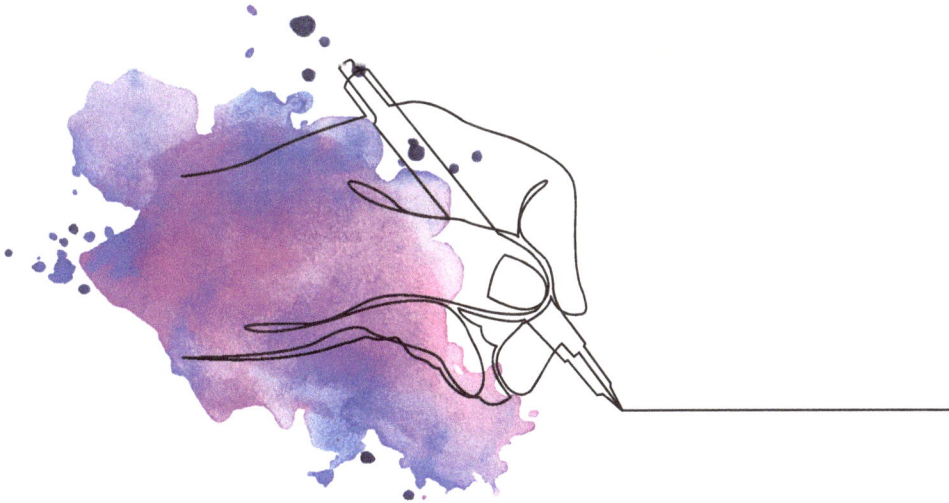

# Writing

Every word

Every experience

Every happening

No matter how it comes

Into consciousness

Is an opportunity

A new piece

A new story

A new musing


Letters float

In my head

Images appear

In my mind's eye

Words emerge

On the screen

Of my inner vision

Sensing the potential

Of magic on the page

# Pyramid

Trust in your soul's destination
Through the four points
Of a pyramid

Charged action and healing
Pyramids are stable and balanced
Amplify attract and manifest

Drawing in personal power
Accepting what is
Changing our consciousness

Opening up
Higher levels of connection
With everything around us

Pure love and grace
As well as compassion
Leads to bliss

Joy and happiness
Along with connection
Brings oneness

Self-discovery and self-acceptance
Including self-love
Allows for peace

Show others how to connect
With oneness
And so learn to feel free

Helping us understand
That in our separation
We are intricately linked

# Ankh

A modified hieroglyph

Cross topped with loop

Key of life

Reproductive organs

Joining masculine and feminine

Gender is irrelevant

Union of opposites

Purifying

Life giving

Procreating

Renewing life

Eternal

Or perhaps greed

All symbols have multiple meanings


Interpretations based on context

Perspective

By the reader

Or the seer

Adding their own experience

To the view

A hue

Train of thought

Of their personality


Like the one who spoke

Of my experience

That I haven't had since 2013

When I let go

Of my past

Took the time

To recreate

My future

A renewal

Giving back my life


Bonding ether

With earth

Divine protection

For all

# Scarab

I felt as if the sun was rising

When my eyes set on it

An Egyptian symbol

Of regeneration

An amulet, or a seal, or jewelry

Representing divine manifestation

Something from nothing

Rebirth

A heavenly cycle

Renewing

Like one day to the next

A new opportunity

To reset

Every time the sun rises

# Tree of life

Twenty-two paths
Frequencies connect
With unknown dimensions
Sacred symbols that rise
From deeper wisdom
We barely comprehend

Holding all of life
Everything it grasps
Endless cycle of creation
Restoring at night
Rising with the sun
Birthing the world

# Water of life

The elixir to extend life
What magic it must contain
Without it we'd be reduced
To 30% of bone and dried matter

We seek the elixir
Yet we consume it day by day
For we can't live for long
Without drinking water

What would it be like
If 30% of what we consumed
Was actually water
We'd find the elixir to extend life

# Wheel of life

Samsara and karma

Working together

Cycles in nature

Series of actions

Sequence of reactions

Periodical events

Daily habits

Repetitions in what we experience

Until we learn the lessons

Grow develop ascend

Peel off layers

And meet the next

Because nothing is permanent

The only certainty

Is change

# Sacred geometry

As above
So below

Shapes take form
Echoes of tunes

As above
So below

Circles pyramids
Mandalas spirals

As above
So below

Conjunction of science
And spirituality

As above

So below


Fibonacci sequence

Golden ratio


As above

So below


Unity in everything

No separation


As above

So below

# Tarot

Cards speak to me
Flashing signs and symbols
Outlining my landing strip
A light house beckoning to land

As if I were searching
For an address on a map
Some meanings I get directly
Immediate flashes of knowledge

I close my eyes
Visions, feelings, tastes fill me
Clues within our reality
Providing direction to the mysteries

Secrets enclosed in the Arcana
Twenty-two Major ones
The mysticism unfolds
Starting as a fool on life's journey

At the turn of the wheel

As we gather lessons from challenges and gains

Seek connection with ourselves and others

An opportunity to look into a mirror of self-reflection


Guidance for the day week month year

Fifty-five Minor ones

Our psyche balanced

By staves, cups, swords, and coins


Provoke passionate and willful fires

Filling cups with soulful feelings

Thoughts that cut through the air

What we gather from the earth

A theme, purpose or answer

In the seventy-eight

The world in our hands

Appears esoteric, mystical, and magical


Representing the human experience

Which is esoteric, mystical, and magical

Archetypal influences

On human nature

# The fates

Three busy ladies

Who weave our fates

Like sweetgrass for a basket

Carefully twisting

For people to meet

Creating circumstances

Place to go

Things to do

People to see

Words to speak

Setting it all

Entwining destiny

By turning the loom

Mere threads

Of our lives

# Spirit

From Latin spiritus
Breath and wind
From Indo European
To blow or to breathe

We all breathe
Soma psyche nous
Nous Pneuma Arché
Soul spirit Holy Spirit

We all breathe

Spiritual must then be

A breathing person

The practice of breathing


We all breathe

The essence of life

Bringing in oxygen

We are all spiritual

# Wisdom says

*Based on Gregg Braden's The Wisdom Codes

Aum is the ultimate name
It was the first sound

The holy sound wasn't born and cannot die
I am part of the melodious flow

I am safe because I am part of a community
It's the basis of compassion

Everything is impermanent
Even harmony is temporary

I lose what I attach to
It wasn't mine to being with

I trust in the universe
A net appears when I leap

There was a purpose for my life
And thus I surrender

I am with God and God is with me
I am not alone

Spiritual energy destroys suffering
Divine light guides me

My soul is eternal
Only my body is not

It's hardest to be the one left behind
When everyone else has moved on

There is beauty in all things
No matter how hard we shut our eyes

Confidence comes when we live from purpose
Or is it the other way around

We heal from within

Only we don't realize the power we hold


I lack nothing

That comforts me


I will

It's my choice


I am

Who else can I be


Lead me to what is real and light

Shanti, shanti, shanti

# Darkness

Instead of living
In deep dark corners
Of our psyche

Move into the light
Step into
A lit balcony

Exposed
For the world to see
We may be

The only ones
Who notice
People are usually

Too busy
Heads stuck in their phones
To look up

At the balcony
And notice us
On it

We feel exposed
But we're not
It isn't about secrets

Even if there are some
It is about the ugly
That lived for too long

Plaguing the darkest
Recesses of our minds
In sharing

We bring them to light
And through that light
Find our own light

# Light

I had a bright shining light
Once
I loved it
I danced in it
I twirled in it
I laughed in it

I miss that light
I don't know where it went
It was there one day
I didn't notice how
It slowly shut down
Gone all of a sudden

A long time passed

Before I noticed

I don't know how long

Because I got used to the dark

Even when I noticed

The light in someone else


I didn't realize

My light was no longer there

I would wonder how they got a light

But I didn't notice mine was out

I didn't remember

I once had one

# Rainbow

I want to chase after it

Find the pot of gold

But I know it's an illusion

Only a sight to cherish

A promise to bloom

Wishes soon to come true

# Vesica piscis

Bladder of the fish

Two intersecting disks

From one came two

Appearing in some form

Christian Roman Greek

Spreading into perfect creation

Buddhist and sacred geometry

Divine opposites

Circular all knowing

Creative force

That made the universe

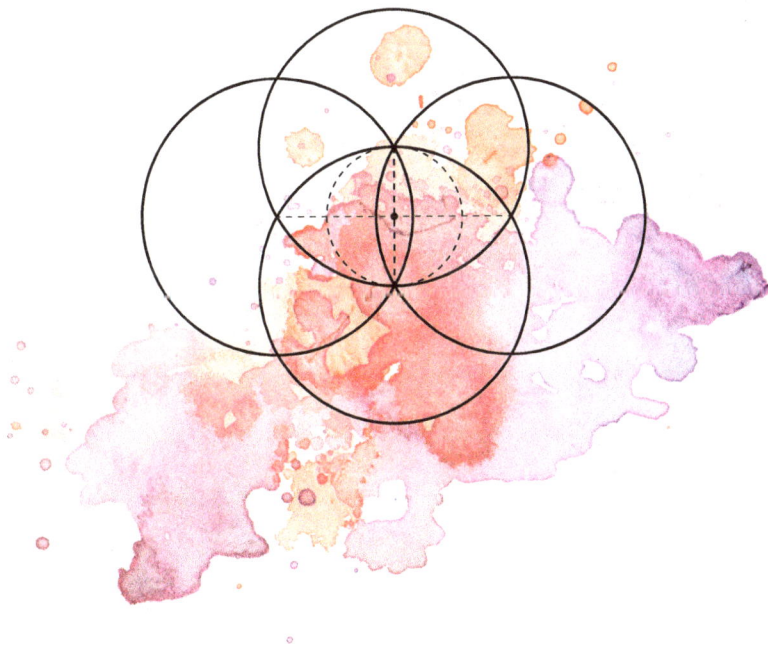

# Elements

Solid earth

Fluid water

Burning fire

Changing wind

Passing space

# Full moon release

In releasing I heal
Letting go is necessary
For all I am going through
All I've been through
Feels less traumatic
The more I do it

I'm left with a desolation
An emptiness of what was
It seeps in every time I release
How much easier would it be
If I didn't experience this at all
How different my life turned out
Than what I expected

I have to refocus

Recalibrate

My life is not meaningless

I do make a difference

In releasing I'm not forgetting myself

I'm merely letting go of my meekness

And embracing my strength


I wake up with renewed purpose

To face the day yet again

Take myself back to the drawing board

Start a new sketch

But it isn't all new

I have been here before

Released many times before


I have grown since then

Learned

Gained a new perspective

I feel the shift

I am ready

To paint a new picture

And release again

Thank you to every single reader. It's for you that I write.

Thank you, Karen. You are a motivation and inspiration and I'm in awe of how you make magic happen.

Thank you, Jennifer. Your cover was exactly what I wanted.

Thank you, Ida. I am amazed by your designs and how you convey the essence of what I'm trying to portray.

Some of these poems have been taken from and/or adapted from poems I posted on social media and published on medium.com. Thank you to all those who liked, hearted, commented and/or shared one of the poems I posted.

Thank you to those who said, "We have a poet in the family," and "I know a poet." They are the best words I've heard so far.

Thank you to my family and friends for all your support.

Thank you, Mama and Papa for your unconditional love and your ongoing belief in me.

# About the Author

Sonee Singh is a cross-cultural seeker of deep knowing. She writes stories of self-discovery to encourage people to accept themselves for who they are and live life on their own terms. Her tales are of her character's definitive moments on their life's journey. The mystical and spiritual are integral in her storytelling, as is her multi-cultural background.

Sonee is of Indian descent, born in Mexico, raised in Colombia, and resides in the United States. When not traveling, reading, or writing, she indulges in meditation, yoga, and aromatherapy.

She holds a Bachelor of Arts in Biology and Society and a Master of Management in Hospitality from Cornell University, and a Master of Science in Complementary Alternative Medicine from American College of Healthcare Sciences. She is currently pursuing a Doctor of Divinity from the University of Metaphysical Sciences.

She worked in hospitality before practicing as a wellness coach. She is certified as an Integrative Nutrition Health Coach, International Certified Health Coach, Reiki Master, Registered Aromatherapist™, Certified Crystal Energy Guide, Certified in Advanced Angel Card Master, and intuitive. These certifications feature in her writing.

Sonee has three poetry books in a collection: *Embody*, *Embrace*, and *Embolden*. She has been published in three anthologies: *Blessing the Page*, *The Colours of Me*, and *The Wishing Stone*. She has multiple articles published on *Elephant Journal*. Her upcoming novel, *Lonely Dove*, will be released in late 2022.

Follow her on **www.soneesingh.com**

www.ingramcontent.com/pod-product-compliance
Lightning Source LLC
Chambersburg PA
CBHW060756150426
42811CB00058B/1424